Stringcraft

By ROLAND
& DOMINIQUE CAURO

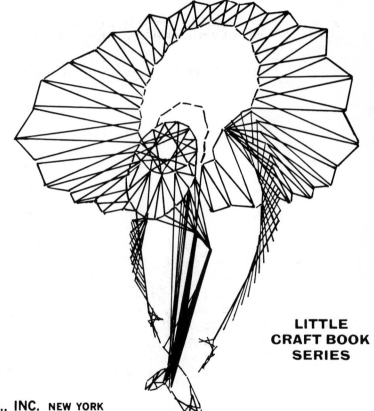

STERLING PUBLISHING CO., INC. NEW YORK

Oak Tree Press Co., Ltd. London & Sydney

Little Craft Book Series

Aluminum and Copper Tooling
Animating Films without a Camera
Appliqué and Reverse Appliqué
Balsa Wood Modelling
Bargello Stitchery
Beads Plus Macramé
Beauty Recipes from Natural Foods
Big-Knot Macramé
Candle-Making
Ceramics by Coil
Ceramics by Slab
Corn-Husk Crafts
Corrugated Carton Crafting
Costumes from Crepe Paper
Crafting with Nature's Materials
Creating from Remnants
Creating Silver Jewelry with Beads
Creating with Beads
Creating with Flexible Foam
Creating with Sheet Plastic
Creative Lace-Making with Thread and Yarn
Cross Stitchery
Decoupage—Simple and Sophisticated

Embossing of Metal (Repoussage)
Felt Crafting
Finger Weaving: Indian Braiding
Flower Pressing
Folding Table Napkins
Greeting Cards You Can Make
Hooked and Knotted Rugs
Horseshoe-Nail Crafting
Ideas for Collage
Inkle Loom Weaving
Junk Sculpture
Lacquer and Crackle
Leathercrafting
Macramé
Making Paper Flowers
Making Picture Frames
Making Shell Flowers
Masks
Metal and Wire Sculpture
Model Boat Building
Monster Masks
Nail Sculpture

Needlepoint Simplified
Net-Making and Knotting
Off-Loom Weaving
Organic Jewelry You Can Make
Patchwork and Other Quilting
Pictures without a Camera
Pin Pictures with Wire & Thread
Puppet-Making
Repoussage
Scissorscraft
Scrimshaw
Sculpturing with Wax
Sewing without a Pattern
Starting with Papier Mâché
Starting with Stained Glass
Stone Grinding and Polishing
Stringcraft
String Designs
String Things You Can Create
Tissue Paper Creations
Tole Painting
Whittling and Wood Carving

Translated by Anne E. Kallem

Originally published in France under the title "Tout l'art des Fils Tendus" by Editions Sélection
J. Jacobs S. A. Paris. ©1975

Copyright © 1976 by Sterling Publishing Co., Inc.
419 Park Avenue South, New York, N.Y. 10016
Distributed in Australia and New Zealand by Oak Tree Press Co., Ltd.,
P.O. Box J34, Brickfield Hill, Sydney 2000, N.S.W.
Distributed in the United Kingdom and elsewhere in the British Commonwealth
by Ward Lock Ltd., 116 Baker Street, London W 1
Manufactured in the United States of America
All rights reserved
Library of Congress Catalog Card No.: 76–1181
Sterling ISBN 0-8069-5364-0 Trade   Oak Tree 7061-2175-9
5365–9 Library

Contents

Before You Begin

Wood, nails and string—this sounds like a list of equipment for a wood-working do-it-yourselfer. But, did you realize that you also can use these materials to compose abstract or realistic pictures? It is not difficult to create distinctive, striking string pictures; children can make simple compositions on their own and even the more difficult constructions—intriguing to crafters of all ages—can be handled by young people if given a little guidance.

This book introduces you to the art of stretched strings. The first pages explain the basic ideas and techniques. Following that are several original patterns for projects you can try, using what you have learned. The illustrations of the finished works also will give you ideas and inspiration for creating designs of your own. So, take a piece of wood, some pins and some string or threads and get started. You will be surprised at how quickly you can master the art of stretched thread.

Materials

Wood

Ordinary wood, plywood, fibrewood or plasterboard can serve as a base in which to anchor pins.

Pins

Next, you need some points—that is, nails (including horseshoe nails), tacks, pins of any sort, with or without heads, and so on. The type of pin you select depends on the project you plan, especially whether you want them to be an obvious part of the design or as invisible as possible. In most cases, you will want to fasten the nails into the board before you paint it, so that you can cover everything at one time with the same color.

Threads

You can use any type of fibre—string, thread, yarn or cord—to create designs. The weight and color of the fibres depend on—and also influence—the type of creation you have in mind. Heavier or coarser fibres lend a different feeling to a project than finer, more elegant types. Consider the effects you wish to create as you consider the various possibilities.

Paint

Paint and a brush, plus a dropcloth or some old newspapers are the only materials you need for coloring the base. If you use a dark shade, any shadows that the threads make on the support will not be so noticeable. Choose flat or glossy colors, as you wish.

Tools

Finally, you need a light hammer, a ruler and a plastic triangle, a fairly large compass, an awl, a pencil, and a gum eraser. A large needle is useful when you place nails very close together.

Preparing the Background

Transferring the Pattern

When you are planning designs of your own, work them out first as small sketches on graph paper. The diagrams for the projects in this book have already been squared off for you. Each square represents 1 inch (25 mm.) in relation to

Illus. 1. First plan your design on a piece of graph paper, as shown here.

Illus. 2. Next, make squares on the background and transfer the design one square at a time.

the size of the actual string picture illustrated, but you can make them larger or smaller, as you wish, by simply transferring them onto larger or smaller squares. The next step is to enlarge these small plans to the actual size of your work and transfer them onto the base. If you are planning to paint the base and nails, draw the design directly onto the raw wood. Make large squares in proportion to the amount of enlargement and transfer the design freehand, one square at a time. If you are going to cover the base with some other material, such as felt, enlarge the pattern to full size on a separate piece of paper. Mark where each nail is to go, lay the paper in position on top of the board, and drive the nails right through the pattern.

Placing the Nails

Depending on the thickness of the nails and the coarseness of the thread, place a nail every $\frac{1}{4}$ or $\frac{1}{2}$ inch (about 5 or 10 mm.) along each line of the

design. Use a pencil or the point of a compass to put marks along every line and curve to indicate the placement of the nails. When two or more lines must have the same number of nails, make a "projection" of the placement marks from one line to the other.

Illus. 3. With a pencil or compass, mark every $\frac{1}{4}$ or $\frac{1}{2}$ inch (5 or 10 mm.) to indicate where to place the nails.

5

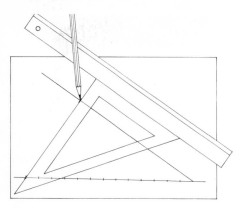

Illus. 4. If two lines in your design have the same number of points, make a "projection" from one line to the other to mark the nail placement.

The accompanying drawing shows an example of projection from line A to line B. Fix your ruler in place with masking tape. Slide the triangle along the ruler. Follow along the edge of the triangle to find the points on line B that correspond to each of the points on line A. Use the point of an awl to mark the placement of each nail on the base.

Illus. 5. Hammer the nails about ¼ inch (5 mm.) into the background. Try to drive them all to an equal depth.

Setting the Nails

You must sink each nail at least ¼ inch (5 mm.) to ensure that the force of several stretched strings pulling on them will not work the nails out of the wood. For the harmony of the picture, drive all the nails to an equal depth.

When all the nails are in place, paint the board and the nails.

Illus. 6 (left). After you have placed all the nails, paint the board and the nails.

Illus. 7 (below). To begin threading, make a slip knot around the nail. Secure it with two simple knots, as shown.

Threading Techniques

Stretch the thread directly from spools without unrolling it first. Hold the spool in the hollow of your hand which serves as a shuttle. It is from the flow of the thread that you create designs. You must, therefore, do this part with great care. Also remember that the whole structure depends upon your attaching the thread firmly to the first pin. Make a slip knot and draw it closed around the nail. Then secure it with two simple knots (a double half hitch). Carefully cut off any excess thread.

Threading an Outline

With this simple technique, you simply run the thread from one nail to another to create the outline of an object or a scene. This technique produces basic forms with the least amount of thread. If you use this technique by itself, choose thick fibres such as coarse wool or raffia for your project.

Illus. 8. To thread, hold the spool in the hollow of your hand, as shown here.

Filling in Areas

Simple Weaving

To weave a thread between two rows of nails, work from one end of the rows to the other. You can double the coverage by weaving back in the opposite direction.

Illus. 9. Run the thread from one nail to the other to thread a simple outline.

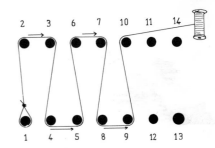

Illus. 10. Simple weaving between two rows of nails.

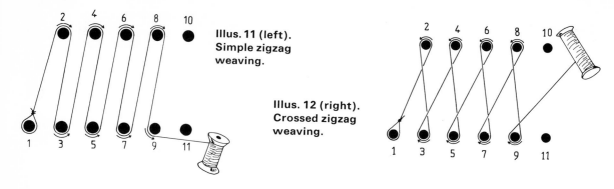

Illus. 11 (left).
Simple zigzag
weaving.

Illus. 12 (right).
Crossed zigzag
weaving.

Zigzags

To fill in areas of a design where you want to create the effect of shadow, for example, or where you want to have the threads make stripes or zebra markings, use zigzag threading. You can use either a simple zigzag (very tight) or a crossed zigzag (more airy). The drawings show examples of each.

Threading More Complex Forms

Circles

If the shape of the area you intend to cover is a closed curve—that is, a circle or an ellipse—proceed as follows:

From the starting nail (1), go to the nail which is diametrically opposite (2). Pass the thread

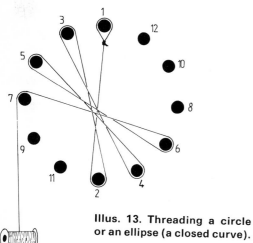

Illus. 13. Threading a circle or an ellipse (a closed curve).

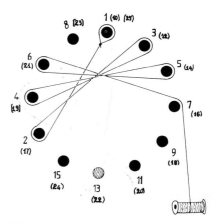

Illus. 14. Threading a ring (a circle with a hole in the middle).

8

around it and come back to the nail (3) next to the starting nail. Continue in this way until you reach, once again, the starting nail. Note that you will pass the thread around each nail twice. All that is left for you to do is to make a final knot on the starting nail.

By varying this technique slightly, you can produce a ring (a circle with a hole in the middle). Following the steps above, starting again with nail 1, but connect it with a nail which is located one, two or more positions to the right or left of the nail directly opposite (in the diagram, the shaded nail is diametrically across, so connect the string with any of the nails marked 9, 11, 15, 2, and so on). Then return to the nail which is next to the starting nail (nail 3 in this case). As before, make two passes around each nail (in the diagram, the numbers in parentheses indicate the second pass of the string). Make the final knot at 25, your return to the starting nail. Note that the inner circle which is formed by the intersecting threads will be near the outer circumference when you connect pins that are close together, but nearer to the midpoint when you connect pins that are farther apart.

Clusters of Rays

Rays from an Axis

This technique allows you to fill in the triangular-shaped area between a row of nails and a single nail which serves as an axis for the rays. Tie a knot around the single nail. With a turning motion, run the thread back and forth between each nail of the line and the axis nail.

This technique has many possible variations.

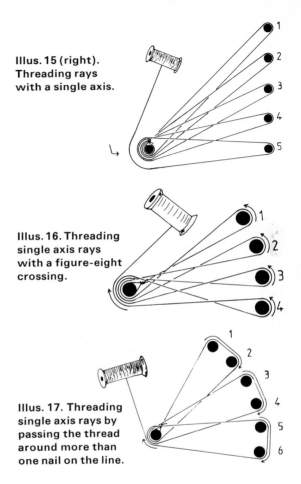

Illus. 15 (right). Threading rays with a single axis.

Illus. 16. Threading single axis rays with a figure-eight crossing.

Illus. 17. Threading single axis rays by passing the thread around more than one nail on the line.

The simplest consists of crossing the string in a figure eight between each of the nails of the line and the axis.

For another variation, you do not pass your thread around just a single nail in the line, but two or more. This variation can also include a figure-eight crossing.

9

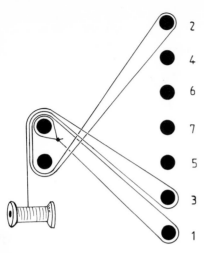

Illus. 18. Threading rays with a double axis.

Rays with a Double Axis

This technique is essentially the same as for a cluster of rays with one axis. You use the two nail axes together, but fasten the beginning knot around only one of them. Here, again, a figure-eight crossing is possible.

Illus. 19. Weaving a curve along two trapezoidal lines.

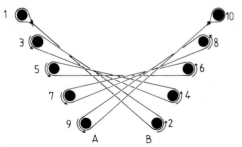

Curves (Parabolas)

With this technique of weaving threads between points along two lines, the intersecting threads form a parabolic curve which you can vary a great deal by changing the relative positions of the lines.

Trapezoidal Lines

If the lines of nails to be connected are trapezoidal, start with a knot on the first nail of one row, then stretch the string to the last nail of the opposite row. Come back to the second nail of the first line, returning then to the next-to-the-bottom nail of the second row. Continue in this manner, connecting all the nails of the two lines. The resulting shape is a form with two straight sides fixed by the rows of nails, a curve and a triangular-shaped wedge created at the top and bottom by the overlapping threads.

Angles

If the two rows of nails meet to form an angle, then the wedge mentioned above disappears and the area is entirely filled in. The process remains the same, but you end up with a three-sided form with a beautiful, sweeping curve created by the overlapping strings on the open side.

Variation of the Angle

The more closed the angle (that is, less than 90°), the smaller the surface area covered and the closer together the intersections of the threads will be. This creates a slender, graceful form. As the angle becomes greater than 90°, the flatter the curve will be.

Up to this point, the curves discussed have been created between two equal rows each having the same number of nails. If the sides of the angle are not the same length, you can use projection (see page 6) to space the same number of nails along each side.

If the lines do not have the same number of nails, you will have to resort to some "trickery." Tie your thread onto the nail at the far end of the longest side. Weave the thread back and forth in the usual manner until you have connected all the nails on the short side to an equal number of nails on the long side. Continue to use the outside nail on the short side (number 12 in the illustration) as the axis for a cluster of rays to the nails remaining on the long side. End with a knot at the axis after passing the string

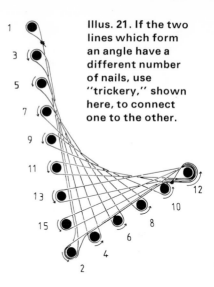

Illus. 21. If the two lines which form an angle have a different number of nails, use "trickery," shown here, to connect one to the other.

around the last nail on the long side. (For an example of this "trickery" process, see the "Perspective" project on page 31.)

Some Variations

Some possible variations of weaving curves are: figure-eight crossing of the string as you thread it; threading from one nail on one side to two nails on the other to avoid "the trick"

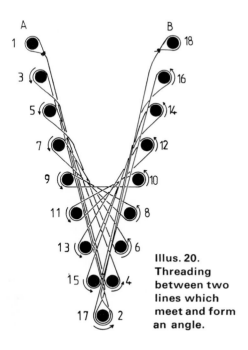

Illus. 20. Threading between two lines which meet and form an angle.

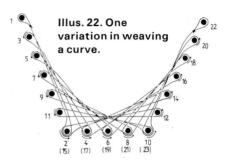

Illus. 22. One variation in weaving a curve.

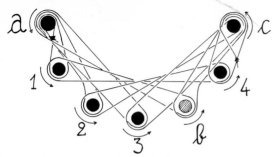

Illus. 23. Weaving a curve between a curved line of nails rather than two straight lines.

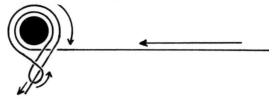

Illus. 24. If two figures within a design require the same color thread, you can connect one to the other. Instead of making a final knot on the first figure, simply continue to the second one. Make a final secure knot at the end of the second figure.

described earlier in the case of sides unequal by half the number of nails; and threading two nails on one side to two nails on the other.

You can also weave curves between nails set in an open curve rather than on two straight lines. Begin as follows: attach the string to one of the outside nails of the curve (a in the illustration). From this nail, stretch the string towards the bottom of the curve in order to find—by trial and error—the first nail of the curve (marked b in the illustration). Having found this nail, run rays between a and each of the nails along the curve between the outside nail a and nail b. When you reach nail b, start weaving the curve by coming back to the nail next to a, returning then to the first nail beyond b. Continue weaving back and forth until you reach nail c. From c, thread rays to the remaining nails of the curve, those that have just a single wrapping of string. (For examples of this threading variation, refer to the bodies of the seal on page 17 and of the shark on page 41.)

You can also use this technique on asymmetrical curved lines. As in the case of unequal lines, it is always easiest to start along the longest part of a curve. For elegance, you can end certain angles in rounds rather than points; proceed as if you were weaving within an open curve. (For an example of this, see the morning glory on page 25.)

Generally, unless you are trying to create a specific effect, do not mix too many variations in a single picture.

Connecting Two Areas

A pattern or design can be made up of several shapes (curves within curves, curves within angles, and so on). For convenience, you can connect one figure to the other. To do this, finish the first figure, but do not make the final knot when you arrive at the last nail. In order to leave this nail, simply begin the next figure. (You can only proceed in this way, of course, if the string is the same color.) Once you have finished threading a string, knot it solidly onto the last nail.

In the examples shown in this book, the threading of the strings starts on the left, but you can begin from the right just as well.

12

Patterns

The remainder of this book is a selection of different patterns, each accompanied by its construction diagram. You should first of all transfer this diagram to your base. To make this easy for you, the diagrams are shown on graph paper with each square representing 1 inch (25 mm.) in actual size. You can make your own picture to a larger or smaller scale simply by transferring the designs onto larger or smaller squares. The construction lines are designated by capital letters (A, B, C, and so on); the reference points for the placement of the nails serving as axes are designated by small letters (a, b, c, and so on), occasionally by numbers.

Once you have learned the basic techniques of stringcraft through making or at least reading through the directions for the specific projects, you will surely want to go on to design original creations of your own. These projects do demonstrate all the skills you will need to make just about any kind of stretched-string picture.

Two Figures

Materials
green paint for the background;
brass nails with round heads;
gold thread (at least two balls);
a circle of white cardboard $1\frac{1}{2}$ inches (4 cm.) in diameter.

To make this elegant, stylized picture, begin with a knot at the top of A. Then, in a clockwise direction, run a cluster of rays from the tip of A to all the other nails on A. Next, weave a curve between A and B. When you reach the intersection of C and B, run a cluster of rays back to those nails of A which received only a single threading. Weave a curve between C and B in a clockwise direction. Then form an incomplete ring in D, connecting with a curve between C

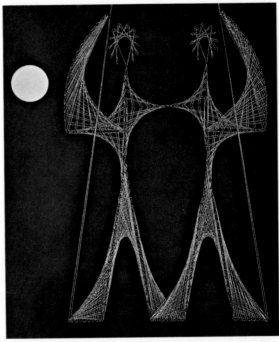

Illus. 25. This project is a good one to familiarize you with the different threading techniques, especially because you do not have to think about changing thread colors as you work.

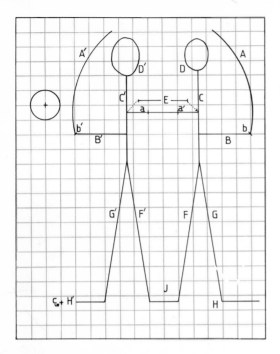

Illus. 26. Pattern for "Two Figures," shown in Illus. 25.

and the right half of E. Weave another curve from the right half of E to the intersection of B and C.

From there, in a clockwise direction, weave a curve between E and the lower part of C. Make a curve between F and J, and finish filling in the space by running a cluster of rays from the end of J to the remaining nails of F. Run your thread back along the bottom of J and then weave a curve between F and G. When you reach the end of G, pass your thread along the bottom of H and run a cluster of rays from the end of H to as many nails on G as you used with the cluster from J to F. Now weave a curve from

H to G, and connect it to a curve between G and the lower part of C and B. Then run your thread along the outside of A, tying off at the top nail.

Follow the same steps for the symmetrical figure, using A', B', C', . . . H', but with each movement in the opposite direction.

Construct lances by threading an outline between two thumbtacks, fastened into the back of the base, and the nails at the bottom left and right of the feet.

Glue on the white circle to complete the picture.

Equilibrium

Black and white threads with their contrast made stronger by painted backgrounds present a striking picture.

Materials
red, white, and black paint;
$\frac{3}{4}$-inch (20-mm.) large-headed tacks.

To prepare the baseboard, apply bright red paint to the area outside of the large circle. Paint the surface between lines A and C plus the small circle E with flat white. Finally, cover the area between C and B and the small circle D with flat black paint.

The threading technique is that of running clusters of rays with their axis at tack a. Start with the black thread that will go over the white-painted area. Knot on at a and thread rays to each of the tacks along line C from point a to point b. Continue threading rays from a to each of the points on line A, passing the thread counterclockwise around the small circle D. Finally, run rays to the points along line C between c and a, tying off when you reach a.

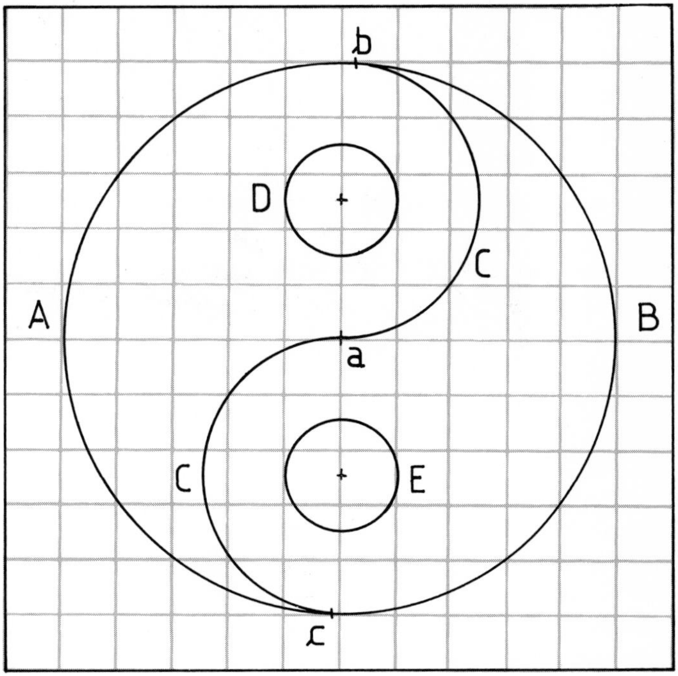

Illus. 27. Pattern for "Equilibrium," shown in Illus. 28.

Illus. 28. You can contrast simple black-and-white threading with a bright background to create an outstanding wall hanging such as the one shown here.

Now use the white thread. Knot on at a and follow the same process as for the black thread, running rays between a and all of the tacks along line C between a and c. Continue threading rays from a to the points along line B, then along C from b back to a.

Fill in circle D with white thread, circle E with black.

Trained Seal

Illus. 29. Use your stringcraft skills to "teach" a graceful seal to balance two balls at once. Your results can easily be as charming as the seal shown here.

Materials
$\frac{5}{8}$-inch (15-mm.) brads;
dark green paint for the background;
white thread for the seal,
orange thread for ball A,
and gold thread for ball B;
cardboard for the eye.

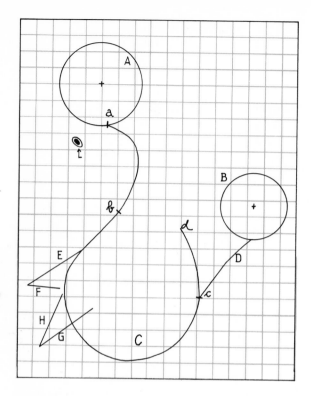

Illus. 30. Pattern for the "Trained Seal," shown in Illus. 29.

Knot on at b and run rays between this point and the nails along C between b and the intersection of C and G. Weave a curve on the points along line C between the intersection of lines C and G and point c. End with a cluster of rays from c to the remaining nails of line C that have been wrapped with thread only once. Knot off at c.

Knot on at point a at the end of C and weave a curve in the angle between line C from d to c and line D. Tie a finish knot at the end of D. Now go to the end of line G and using "trickery" (see page 11), weave a curve in the angle between G and H.

From the end of H, wind your thread round the last nail of F and use this point as the axis for running a cluster of rays to the 5 nails of E closest to the intersection of E and F. Then weave a curve to the end of E. Make a final knot at this nail.

Complete your picture with an eye cut from a piece of cardboard and drawn in with ink.

Transfer the design to your base. Place 32 nails at equal distances from one another around circle A, 25 nails around circle B, 9 nails along lines E and G, 8 nails on line H, and 19 nails along line D. Place 69 nails along line C.

To make balls A and B, thread them as circles (see page 8).

Next, make a knot at a and run rays from a to all the nails along line C between points a and b. Weave a curve along line C up to the intersection of C and E. Knot off at this nail.

Jalopy

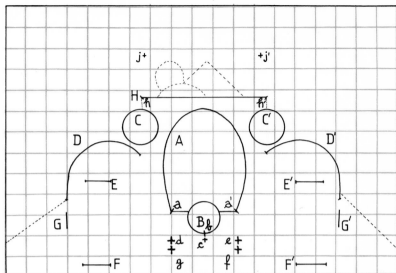

Illus. 31. Pattern for the "Jalopy," shown in Illus. 32.

Putting together a jalopy like this one is not difficult. Car lovers will enjoy it and so will anyone else.

Materials

acrylic paints—blue for the sky, green for the car body and the road, greenish brown for the tree, white for the face and the clouds;

$\frac{5}{8}$-inch (15-mm.) flat-headed steel nails for lines D, E, F, D′, E′, and F′;

brass nails with round heads for all other lines;

white and red thread;

thin brass wire or gold-colored twine.

With the white thread, tie onto the nail at the left end of E and thread an outline from left to right between the points on lines E and F. When you reach the end of the line, thread back in the opposite direction. Follow the same procedure between the points on lines E′ and F′. Run a cluster of rays from b out to the points on G and then to the points on G′. Repeat from point c. Thread an outline several times around points a–c–e–f–g–d.

Now tie the red thread on at a. Run a cluster of rays from a to the nails along line D. To fill in the area more solidly, run a second set of rays between these points, but this time cross the string in a figure eight between the axis and each of the nails. Do the same thing between point a′ and the nails on line D′.

Before continuing with the red thread, pair off the middle nail on line A with the middle nail on line H. Tie on to the middle nail and work towards the left, weaving the thread back and forth between the nails on the two lines. For the last 6 nails of H, connect 2 nails of H with one

Illus. 32. Can you picture yourself driving such a fancy old jalopy? Why not use a photograph of yourself to form the driver to make this dream come true?

of A. Start again at the middle nail and work towards the right in the same manner. You can see this clearly in the color illustration.

Next, work with the gold thread. Fill in the circles B, C, and C′, then outline their outer edges. Thread an outline around h–j–j′–h′, then back again in the opposite direction to form a double border. For the radiator, match up nails again starting from the middle so that you can thread lines that are vertical and equidistant. Finally outline the radiator with gold thread and your jalopy is ready for the road!

Parrot

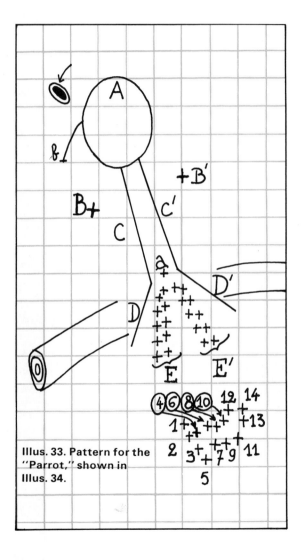

Illus. 33. Pattern for the "Parrot," shown in Illus. 34.

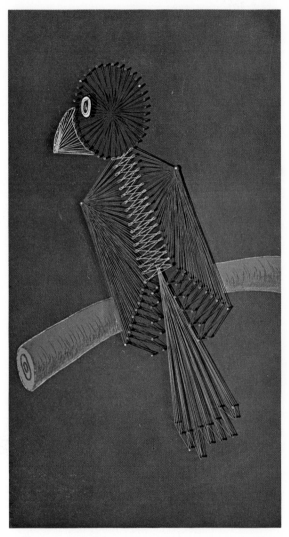

Illus. 34. An exotically colored parrot such as this one certainly brings the tropics to mind.

This colorful parrot may not talk, but it will always add a bright splash of color to any room.

Materials
$\frac{5}{8}$-inch (15-mm.) nails;
a dark acrylic paint for the background, a lighter color paint to be accented with crayon for the branch;
cardboard eye drawn in with India ink;
red, yellow, green and turquoise threads.

To begin, form the head from red thread by filling in circle A. Next, using the yellow thread, make a beak by running a cluster of rays from b to those nails of A facing b.

With the turquoise thread, make the tail—a simple cluster of rays run from a to each of the nails numbered from 1 to 14. Then use turquoise to thread an outline from 14 to 1.

Make the wings from green thread. Run a cluster of rays from point B to the nails along lines C and D. Do the same from point B' to the lines C' and D'.

Next, fill in the wing-tips with red thread. First make a simple zigzag between lines D and E, then return to create a crossed zigzag. Do the same between D' and E' and back again.

Using yellow thread, make the parrot's back with a simple zigzag between C and C'. Work from top to bottom, then return to make a crossed zigzag.

Glue on the cardboard eye, draw in the branch and your parrot is finished.

The Crow and the Fox

Materials
green acrylic for the background, greenish brown for the branch;
wool cord (or braid) in black, yellow, brown and off-white;
$\frac{3}{4}$-inch (20-mm.) tacks;
cardboard or felt to make the eyes.

Crow

After you paint the background and add the branch, start work on the crow. Begin with the black cord. For the tail, knot on at one end of F. Weave a curve between F and G. Make a knot at the end of G.

To make the body, knot on at a, then run rays from a to the nails on A, continuing down the lower section of B, around H and back to the branch. Make an end knot at a.

To make the head, knot on at the end of C, and run rays to all the nails of B and of E. Tie off at the end of C.

Using the yellow cord to make the beak, simply weave a curve between D and E. The tongue is a curve between C and D. Finally, using the off-white cord, make the cheese in the crow's mouth. Simply fill in the circle H.

Fox

Now make the hungry-looking fox. With some brown wool or cord, knot on at the end of

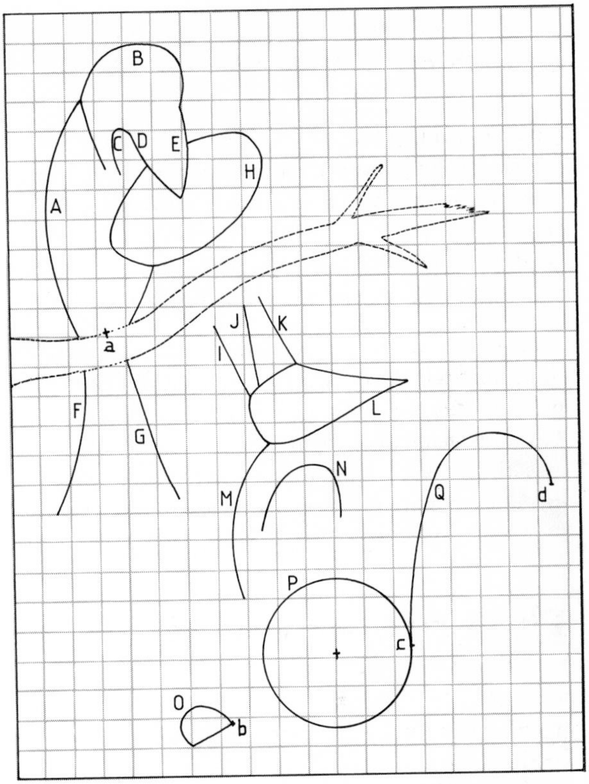

Illus. 35. Pattern for "The Crow and the Fox,"
shown in Illus. 36.

I and weave a curve between I and J. Then, from the top nails of J and K—used as a double axis—run a cluster of rays to L to form the muzzle. Then make a ring within L by connecting pins seven spaces apart to make the head itself (see page 9).

From the fifth nail of N, counting from the left, run a cluster of rays to M. When you reach the bottom of line M, connect it with b. Fill in the form O as you would a circle. Then, from point b run rays to the nails on N. Starting at nail c, fill in the circle P with a double thread. When you come back to c for the second time, run rays to the first 15 nails of Q, counting from c. Then weave a curve from there to d, from which point you then run rays back to the nails of Q that have only one wrapping of thread. Make an end knot at d.

All that is left is to glue on the eyes which you draw with ink on felt or thin cardboard.

Illus. 36. This hungry fox and greedy crow tell a picture story which might remind you of a fairy tale you know. It is easy and fun to illustrate fables using the stringcraft techniques.

Morning Glory

Illus. 37. You can make a beautiful dimensional flower by weaving several layers one on top of the other, as was done to create this magnificent morning glory.

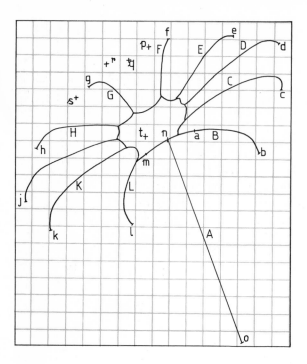

For this project, be sure to make a knot at the end of each curve.

Start by knotting on the violet cord at point o. Weave a curve between the nails on line B from n to a and an equal number of nails at the bottom of line A. When you reach a, run rays to the remaining nails of A. Make an end knot at a. Now do the same operation between A and the points on L from n to m.

Next form the petals. You make each petal from three layers of threads in the following order: purple, violet, dusty rose. All of the curves making up the petals start out with a cluster of rays from one apex, then a curve woven between nails set along the curved line, and finally another cluster of rays run back from the last nail to those nails along the curve left with only one wrapping of thread. The purple curve will be the shallowest, the dusty rose the deepest.

To finish this multi-layered flower, paint the nails p, q, r and s yellow. Tie p and q to n with yellow thread, then tie r to t and s to m.

Using stringcraft techniques, you can make a morning glory that will stay open all day long.

Materials
green paint for the background;
twisted cord—two spools of violet, two spools of purple, one spool of dusty rose;
yellow thread;
$\frac{5}{8}$-inch (15-mm.) round-headed brass tacks and four $\frac{3}{4}$-inch (20-mm.) flat-headed nails. (Sink the nails along line A deeper than those of the other lines.)

Butterfly

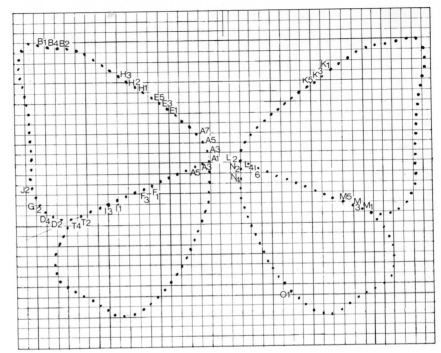

Illus. 39. Pattern for the "Butterfly," shown in Illus. 40.

This project will look colorful and lively hanging on a wall. You can make the string picture even more unusual by cutting the wooden base into a butterfly form.

Materials
a sheet of graph paper;
a piece of thin copper or cardboard for the body;
some $\frac{5}{8}$-inch (15-mm.) nails;
flat black paint for the wood;
orange, rose, yellow and white thread.

Make the body and the antennae from the piece of copper or cardboard. Be sure to cut it

so that the size of the body is in proportion to the wings. Transfer the pattern shown here onto a piece of graph paper, making it the actual size of the finished piece. Lay the pattern on top of the board and pound the nails in right through the paper. Pull the paper away when all the nails are in place.

First work with the orange thread, in two stages. Knot on at A1, go up to B2, return to A3, go up to B4, return to A5, go to B6, return to A7 and continue in this manner until you come back to B2. Make an end knot and cut the thread.

Attach the thread at A1, go just to D2, return

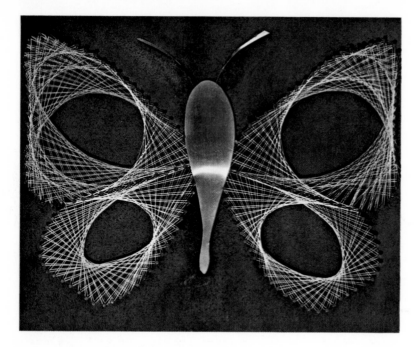

to A3, go to D4, return to A5 and continue in this manner until you come back again to D2. Make an end knot at D2.

The rose thread is also worked in two parts. Attach the thread at E1, go to B2, return to E3, go to B4 and continue in this manner up to B2. Attach the thread and cut. Next, attach the thread to F1, go to G2, back to F3 and again continue to G2. Make an end knot at G2.

Work the yellow thread also in two parts for the upper section of the wing. Attach the thread at H1, go to B4, back to H2, to B6, back to H3 and continue in this manner up to B4. Attach the thread and cut. Attach the thread at I1, go

to J2, back to I3 and continue up to J2. Make an end knot at J2.

Finally, to make the bottom part of the wing, attach the yellow thread at A1, go to T2, return to A3, go to T4 and continue similarly to A1.

Repeat all of the above steps in reverse to form the opposite wing.

Attach the white thread at K1, and weave a curve by going to L2, returning to K3, going to L4, returning to K5, going to L6 and continuing in this manner up to L2. At L2, turn around the nail, go to M1, over to N2, back up to M3, back to N4, to M5, continuing to O1. Make an end knot at O1.

Lion

Materials
$\frac{5}{8}$-inch (15-mm.) flat-headed nails;
brown and off-white raffia;
brown and golden-yellow thread;
bright green, olive and brown acrylics;
some fine sand.

The partially textured background adds special interest to this starry-eyed lion.

Begin this project by painting the upper part of the board green. Spread glue on the lower part of the board, then sprinkle sand over the glue. Paint the sand with touches of the olive and brown paints.

Start the threading by tying the brown thread

Illus. 41. This playful lion looks more friendly than ferocious. By following the directions on this page and the next, you can make this pleasant creature with very little effort.

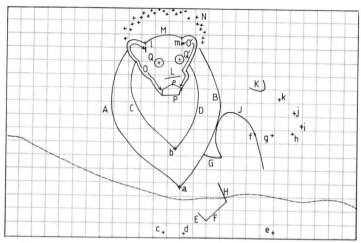

on at o. Run a cluster of rays from o to line P. Using the "trick" described on page 11, weave curves between the points on line o and line M, M and O', O' and o, then o and O.

With the yellow thread, fill in the circles Q and Q' to form the eyes.

Next, work with the brown raffia to run rays from a alternately to one nail of A and to one nail of B, using the first 7 nails of A and of B. Then make a cluster of rays with a as the axis, going round the first nails of A and of B plus, in each case, the next following nail of A and of B. Repeat this same operation running the raffia from a alternately along the outside edge to the next two nails on A and B then back to a, continuing in succession until the outer mane is filled in.

Follow this same threading scheme with the off-white raffia between b and the nails flanking it on C and D.

To form the lion's front legs, use raffia to run clusters of rays from c to the seventh, sixth, fifth, fourth, and third nails to the left of a on line A. Do the same operation between point d and the first, second, third, fourth and fifth nails to the right of a along line B.

Now weave, with brown raffia, from the first nail of L around the first two nails of M, continuing until you reach the end of both lines.

Weave a brown raffia curve between the points on lines E and H, another between lines F and G. Then run a cluster of rays between line G and the nail at the intersection of J and B to complete one of the rear legs. Run another cluster of rays between line J and point e to form the other rear leg. To make the tail, thread an outline around points f–g–h–i–j–k. From point k, run a cluster of rays to the points on line K. Retrace the outline between k and f.

To finish this artful lion, thread a simple zigzag between the points on lines N and M.

Perspective

Repeating forms within similar forms creates the illusion of depth.

Materials
royal blue and sky blue acrylic paints for the background;

twisted cord—2 spools of red, 2 spools of pink and one spool of white.

Start by knotting on the red cord at a. Then weave a curve between A and the right-hand portion of B until you reach b, from where you run rays to the remaining nails of A. From b,

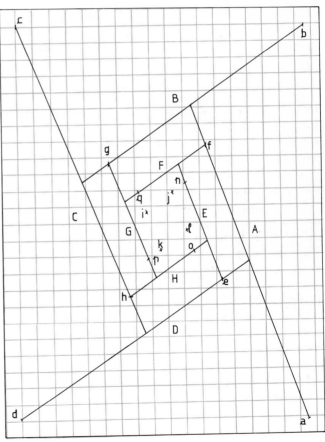

Illus. 43. Pattern for "Perspective," shown in Illus. 44.

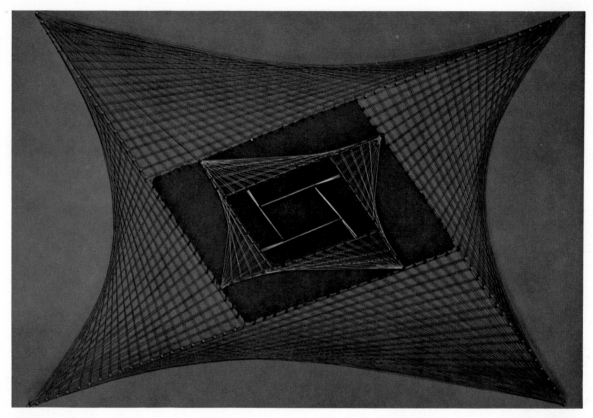

Illus. 44. Abstract designs are striking when created with the stringcraft techniques. This is only one example of the type of effect you can create with a non-realistic pattern.

weave a curve between B and the top section of C until you reach c, from where you stretch rays back to the remaining nails of B. Repeat the same operations between C and D, and between D and A. Make an end knot at a.

With the pink thread, knot on at e. Then form a curve between E and F until you reach f, from where you run rays to the remaining nails of E. Repeat the same procedure between F and G, G and H, and H and E. Make an end knot at e.

With the white thread, knot on at o. Make the following circuit three times: o–j–n–i–q–k–p–l–o. Make an end knot at o.

Sailboat

Illus. 45. Simple curves in the basic shape of a sailboat resulted in this lovely vessel. Graceful, painted seagulls add a special finishing touch to the picture.

Materials
brown and turquoise thread;
light brown raffia;
flat-headed $\frac{5}{8}$-inch (15-mm.) steel nails.

Begin with the brown thread. Run a cluster of rays from a to each one of the nails along line A between b and c. Pass all of the threads to the right of nail b. Knot at c. Run a cluster of rays from h

33

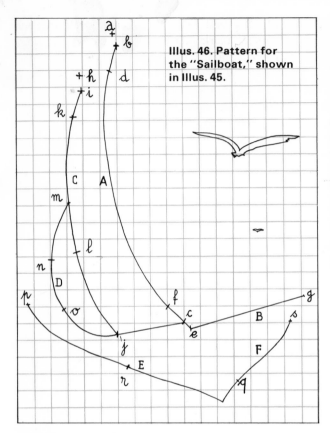

Illus. 46. Pattern for the "Sailboat," shown in Illus. 45.

Illus. 47. Even simple shapes, such as this flower, look intricate when you make them with stringcraft.

to each of the nails of C, from i to j. Pass all of the threads to the right of nail i. Knot at j.

With the turquoise thread, knot on at d. Run rays from d to each one of the nails of A as far as point f, then weave a curve with B up to g. Make a knot at g. Knot on at k and run a cluster of rays from k to each one of the nails of C up to j. Then weave a curve with the line from j to c. Make an end knot at c.

Knot on at m. Run rays from m to each of the nails of D up to o, then weave a curve up to point j. Run rays from j to the remaining nails of C. Make an end knot at j.

With the brown raffia knot on at p, run rays from p to all the nails of E, then to those of F as far as q. Continue with weaving a curve as far as s. Then run rays from s to the remaining nails of E up to the intersection of E with F. Make a final knot at s. Paint on a white seagull or two to add the final nautical touch to this creation.

34

Flower

Materials
$\frac{3}{4}$-inch (2-cm.) nails;
flat black paint for the wood.

Use a compass, a 60° T-square and a ruler or a draftsman's T to construct this project. Trace a 10-inch (25-cm.) square, divide it into 4 equal parts with your T-square, trace the lines AB and BC; then trace the lines CD and EF. Then make a mark on each of these lines at a point 3 inches (7.5 cm.) out from the middle. A compass is a big help in this task. Departing from these marks, trace AH and EH, CI and GI, FJ and BJ, DK and HK. Then draw lines AL and CL, GM and FM, BN and DN, HO and EG. With your compass, mark points on each of the diamond shapes from the midpoint to EHA and similar at intervals of $\frac{7}{16}$ inch (11 mm.). Mark the lines HOE and similar at intervals of $\frac{3}{8}$ inch (10 mm.). After having made all the lines on the paper, lay it over the board and sink the nails. Remove the paper, paint the board, let it dry, and apply another coat of paint if necessary.

With the thread, tie on at the middle nail, go to 1, come back to 2, go to 3, return to 4 and continue in this manner back to your starting point. Do the same for the other side and for the other petals.

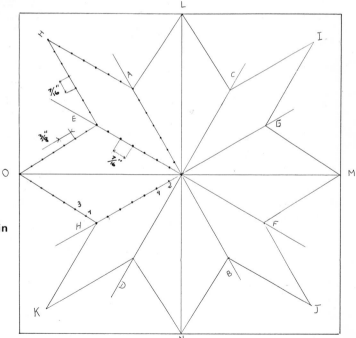

Illus. 48. Pattern for the "Flower," shown in Illus. 47.

Dancer

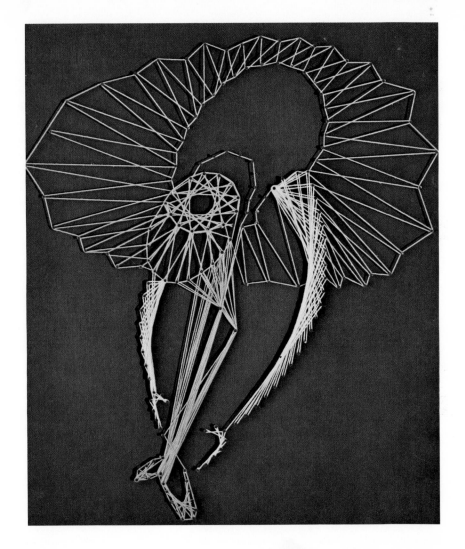

Materials

flat black paint for the background;
off-white, light blue and yellow (or gold) braid;
$\frac{5}{8}$-inch (15-mm.) flat-headed steel nails.

Begin with the light blue braid. Knot on at a. Then do a simple zigzag connecting every other nail on A to a nail with an uneven number, beginning with 1. When you reach 29, go to the nail at the intersection of D with C. Run your thread along the outside of C up to the second nail to the left of 41 on C. From this nail go on to 30, and then make the circuit 30–41–31–42–32. Join 32 to the third nail to the left of a. From here, make the circuit 33–34–third nail of F above 33–37–fifth nail of F above 33–39–a. Make an end knot at a.

Knot on at the first nail above 33. Then do a simple zigzag threading around to the following circuit: first nail above 33–34–third nail above 33–36–fifth nail above 33–38–seventh nail above 33–40–first nail of A to the right of a. Going on from this nail, continue threading from the even-numbered nails to those nails on A that you did not use previously in threading to the odd-numbered nails. Run your thread around A and K, connecting each nail in turn to form these lines. Make an end knot at a.

Knot on at 30 and outline the tutu by running the thread from one nail to the next in numerical order from 30 to 40. Continue by connecting nails 1 to 29 in sequence. Make an end knot at 29.

Knot on at 45. Run a cluster of rays between 45 and the 6 nails of C to the left of 41. From the first nail to the left of 41 on C, carry your thread to 46 and use this as an axis for running rays to points 41, 44, 47 and 48 with all threads passing to the right of 43. Next weave a curve between the two sides of J. Using the first 6 nails of C to the left of 41, run rays to 46 with all of the threads passing to the right around nail 44. Go from 46 to 45 and weave a curve between the two sides of H.

With the off-white braid, weave a "trick"

curve on D and the two nails of C to the right of 29 (with the axis of the cluster of rays on 49). Go on to weave a "trick" curve on E (with the axis for the cluster of rays on 47). Make an end knot at 47.

Now weave a "trick" curve between the 3 nails to the left of a and the points of line F (with the axis of the rays on the third nail to the left of a and on 50). Then continue with a "trick" curve on G. Knot off at 48.

With the yellow or gold braid, fill in the circle B. Connect C and the portion of B included between the ends of C with a crossed zigzag.

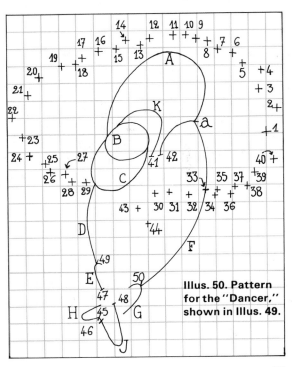

Illus. 50. Pattern for the "Dancer," shown in Illus. 49.

City Skyline

Illus. 51. Straight outlining is a quick and easy way to illustrate a city of your choice using the stringcraft techniques.

Materials
dark blue paint for the background;
headless $\frac{5}{8}$-inch (15-mm.) steel nails;
white twisted cord.

Since this design is composed entirely of straight lines, you can produce it with nothing more than the outline technique. Take a turn around each nail as you work to avoid having the thread come loose later on.

Proceed in the following order:

Outline between C and D, then run the thread along C.

Outline between E and F, then run the thread along E.

Outline between G and H, then run the thread along G.

Outline between J and L, then run the thread along J.

Outline between L and M, then run the thread along L.

Outline between N and O, then run the thread along N.

Now, knot on at 1. Simply stretch the thread between 1, 2, 3, 4, 5, 6, 7, 8, 9, 10, 11, 12, and 13, wrapping the thread once around each nail.

Knot on at 3. Stretch the thread between 3, 14, 15, 16, and 4.

Knot on at 2. Stretch the thread between 2, 14, and 2.

Knot on at 17. Stretch the thread between 17, 18, 19, 20, 21, 22, and 19.

Knot on at 18. Stretch the thread between 18, 23, 24, 25, 26, 27, 28, and 29.

Knot on at 17. Stretch the thread between 17, 23, 24, 27, 24, 31 (a thumbtack on the back), 24, 23, and 17.

Knot on at 9. Stretch the thread between 9, 30, and 9.

Place four nails for each of the roadway openings through the middle of the bridge supports and stretch a thread around them.

Finish this project by threading in the outline of the buildings. Tie on at one end of A and weave from one nail to the one following (above, below or next to) it. Do the same for B.

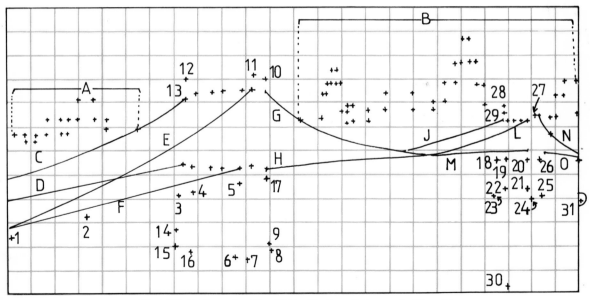

Illus. 52. Pattern for the "City Skyline," shown in Illus. 51.

Shark

You can capture a shark's grace as well as its power by following the directions for this picture.

Materials
flat black paint for the background;
$\frac{3}{4}$-inch (20-mm.) tacks;
silver cord.

Begin with a knot at a. Then make a cluster of rays from a, to the other nails of A up to point d. Weave a curve to b. From b, run a cluster of rays to those nails of A which have only a single thread wrapped around them. Make an end knot at b.

Knot on at c. From c, run a cluster of rays along B almost up to point b. Continue by weaving a curve until you reach e. From there, stretch rays back to those nails of B which only

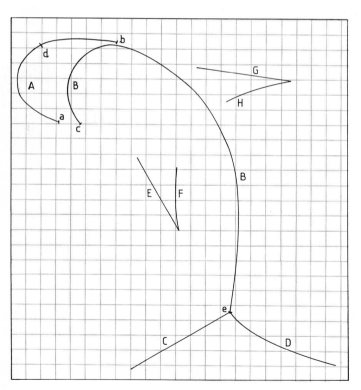

Illus. 53. Pattern for the "Shark," shown in Illus. 54.

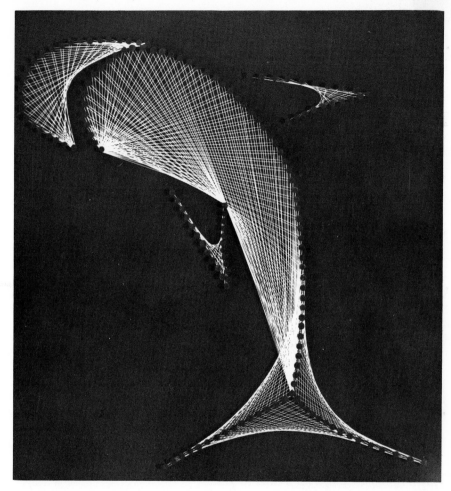

Illus. 54. It is not difficult to feel the grandeur and power of a shark by viewing this version. If you use silver cord, as was done for the shark pictured here, you can also capture some of the shimmering nature of a shark's body.

have a single thread wrapped round them. Make an end knot at e.

Knot on at the bottom of C, and weave a curve between C and D. From the bottom tip of D, weave a curve between D and the corresponding number of nails on B. Also make a curve between B and C. Make an end knot at the bottom tip of C.

Weave a curve between E and F, and another between G and H.

Clown

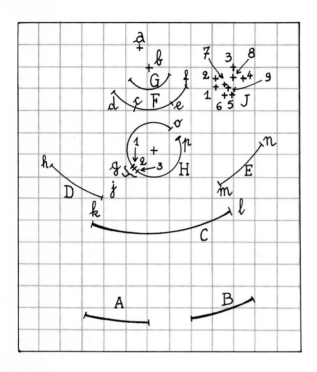

Illus. 55. Pattern for the "Clown," shown in Illus. 56.

What more appropriate project is there than a clown to decorate a child's room? This happy clown is simple enough for a child to make.

Materials
dark blue paint for the background;
off-white cotton braid;
cardboard for the hands, the face with the hat, and the quarter moon;

$\frac{5}{8}$-inch (15-mm.) flat-headed steel nails and two $\frac{3}{4}$-inch (20-mm.) broad-headed nails (for a and b).

Knot on at the outside end of A and make a crossed zigzag between A and the left half of C. Continue from the middle of C with a crossed zigzag between B and the right half of C. Then outline the following circuit twice: l–k–c–d–h–j– c–e–f–n–m–e–l. Start a third circuit as far as d,

42

then connect F and G with a crossed zigzag. Knot off at the right end of G.

Knot on at o. Then weave a curve within H, beginning by uniting o and the fourth nail to the left of g1. When you reach p, run your thread back around the outside of H to o. Then make the circuit from o to J1–J2–J3–J4–J5–J6, then back to p, where you make a knot.

Knot on at g1, and make the following circuit: g1–J7–g1–g2–J8–g2–g3–J9–g3. Make an end knot at g3.

To finish, decorate a cardboard face and hat as you wish. Glue them onto the heads of nails a and b. Make the hands and glue them to the edges of D and E. Make the quarter moon gold, and glue it into the sky.

Illus. 56. Making this clown can be a cheerful way to spend an afternoon. Imagine brightening a gloomy day with this smiling face.

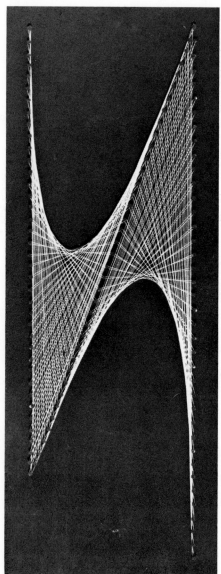

Lightning Bolt

This string picture, which looks like a flash of lightning, stands out against an orange background. The thread used for this picture is violet, but you can use any color you wish. Pattern lines A, B, and C each have 39 $\frac{5}{8}$-inch (15-mm.) flat-headed nails along them. Once you have spaced the nails equally along line A, you can work out the spacing on line B by projection (see page 6), and then on line C. Weave curves within each of the angles.

Illus. 57 (left). You can almost hear the thunder clapping as you create this bright flash of lightning on a board.

Illus. 58 (right). Pattern for the "Lightning Bolt," shown in Illus. 57.

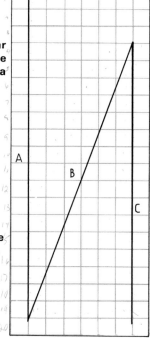

Contrasts

This abstract picture vividly presents the contrast between black and white. It is composed entirely of curves woven within angles.

To make this project, place 15 $\frac{5}{8}$-inch (15-mm.) tacks along lines A, B, C, A', B', and C' (the corner tack counts in both lines). All other lines have 11 tacks. Where lines with the same number of tacks are of unequal length, use projection to determine placement.

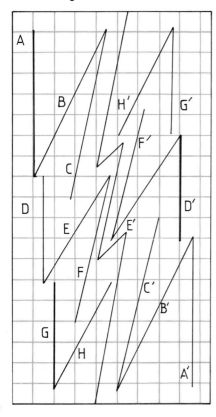

Illus. 59 (right). You can use black and white, or simply light and dark, to produce the striking effect shown here.

Illus. 60 (left). Pattern for "Contrasts," shown in Illus. 59.

Chalet

This pattern calls for a string outline and some zigzag threading.

Materials
$\frac{5}{8}$-inch (15-mm.) long nails;
green, red and brown thread or yarn;
sky blue and white acrylic paints.

To begin, paint the background following the jagged skyline in the drawing—that is, paint the base white and the sky blue. Use masking tape to keep the dividing line sharp.

Use the green thread to make the pine tree. Knot on the thread at 1. Do simple zigzag threading from 1 to 2, 2 to 3, and so on, to nail 15, then go from 15 back to 1. Make an end knot at 1.

Using the brown thread next, make the walls of the chalet. Knot on at A. Thread an outline from A to H in alphabetical order, then go from H back to G and from G to I. Make an end knot at I.

Use the red thread to make the roof. Knot on at A. Thread from a to l in alphabetical order, then from l to i, from i back to l, from l down to g, from g to m, from m to k, from k back to m, and from m to c. Make an end knot at c.

Using red thread again, make the windows following the illustrations. Use the same threading sequence for all three windows. Knot on at 1. Thread in numerical order from 1 to 5, then from 5 to 1, from 1 to 4, from 4 to 6, from 6 to 7, from 7 to 5, from 5 to 6, from 6 to 9, from 9 to 8, and from 8 to 7. Make an end knot at 7.

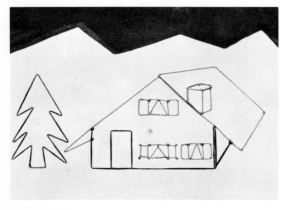

Illus. 61. Not much time, and very few materials, are all you need to create a cozy winter chalet like the one pictured here.

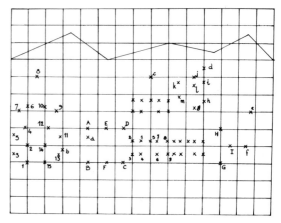

Illus. 62. Pattern for the "Chalet," shown in Illus. 61.

46

Hen

Stylized farm animals are fun to create using the stringcraft technique.

Materials
yellow paint for the base;
brown raffia;
$\frac{5}{8}$-inch (15-mm.) flat-headed nails.

To make this picture, tie the raffia on at a, then go from a to b. Continue by stretching the raffia back and forth between the points along lines D and C until you reach e. Go on by connecting the points along lines E and F until you reach f. Go up to g at the bottom of line B, then around h connecting the points along lines A and B, ending at point a. Finally, double back to h and make an end knot.

Illus. 63. With a little imagination, you can represent many familiar animals—such as this hen—in unfamiliar and creative ways with stringcraft.

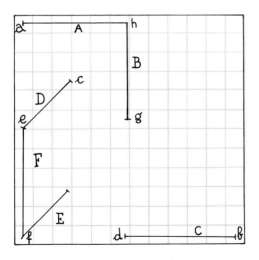

Illus. 64 (left). Pattern for the "Hen," shown in Illus. 63.

Index